the everyman series

being God's man...

in tough times

Real Men. Real Life. Powerful Truth.

D0180675

Stephen Arterburn

Kenny Luck & Todd Wendorff

WATERBROOK
PRESS

BEING GOD'S MAN...IN TOUGH TIMES
PUBLISHED BY WATERBROOK PRESS
12265 Oracle Boulevard, Suite 200
Colorado Springs, Colorado 80921
A division of Random House, Inc.

ISBN 1-57856-679-7

Published in association with the literary agency of Alive Communications, Inc., 7680 Goddard Street, Suite 200, Colorado Springs, CO 80920, www.alivecommunications.com.

Printed in the United States of America
2006

10 9 8 7 6 5 4

contents

welcome to the every man
Bible study series

As Christian men, we crave true-to-life, honest, and revealing Bible study curricula that will equip us for the battles that rage in our lives. We are looking for resources that will get us into our Bibles in the context of mutually accountable relationships with other men. But like superheroes who wear masks and work hard to conceal their true identities, most of us find ourselves isolated and working alone on the major issues we face. Many of us present a carefully designed public self, while hiding our private self from view. This is not God's plan for us.

Let's face it. We all have trouble being honest with ourselves, particularly in front of other men.

As developers of a men's ministry, we believe that many of the problems among Christian men today are direct consequences of an inability to practice biblical openness—being honest about our struggles, questions, and temptations—and to connect with one another. Our external lives may be in order, but storms of unprocessed conflict, loss, and fear are eroding our resolve to maintain integrity. Sadly, hurting Christian men are flocking to unhealthy avenues of relief instead of turning to God's Word and to one another.

We believe the solution to this problem lies in creating opportunities for meaningful relationships among men. That's why we designed this Bible study series to be thoroughly interactive. When a man practices biblical openness with other men, he moves from secrecy to candor, from isolation to connection, and from pretense to authenticity.

Kenny and Todd developed the study sessions at Saddleback Church in Lake Forest, California, where they teach the men's morning Bible studies. There, men hear an outline of the Bible passage, read the verses together, and then answer a group discussion question at their small-group tables. The teaching pastor then facilitates further discussion within the larger group.

This approach is a huge success for many reasons, but the key is that, deep down, men really do want close friendships with other guys. We don't enjoy living on the barren islands of our own secret struggles. However, many men choose to process life, relationships, and pressures individually because they fear the vulnerability required in small-group gatherings. *Suppose someone sees behind my carefully constructed image? Suppose I encounter rejection after revealing one of my worst sins?* Men willingly take risks in business and the stock market, sports and recreation, but we do not easily risk our inner lives.

Many church ministries are now helping men win this battle, providing them with opportunities to experience Christian male companionship centered in God's Word. This study series aims to supplement and expand that good work around the country. If these lessons successfully reach you, then they will also reach every relationship and domain that you influence. That is our heartfelt prayer for every man in your group.

how to use this study guide

As you prepare for each session, first review the **Key Verse** and **Goals for Growth,** which reveal the focus of the study at hand. Discuss as a group whether or not you will commit to memorizing the Key Verse for each session. The **Head Start** section then explains why these goals are necessary and worthwhile. Each member of your small group should complete the **Connect with the Word** section *before* the small-group sessions. Consider this section to be your personal Bible study for the week. This will ensure that everyone has spent some time interacting with the biblical texts for that session and is prepared to share responses and personal applications. (You may want to mark or highlight any questions that were difficult or particularly meaningful, so you can focus on those during the group discussion.)

When you gather in your small group, you'll begin by reading aloud the **Head Start** section to remind everyone of the focus for the current session. The leader will then invite the group to share any questions, concerns, insights, or comments arising from their personal Bible study during the past week. If your group is large, consider breaking into subgroups of three or four people (no more than six) at this time.

Next get into **Connect with the Group,** starting with the **Group Opener.** These openers are designed to get at the heart of each week's lesson. They focus on how the men in your group relate to the passage and topic you are about to discuss. The group leader will read the opener for that week's session aloud and then facilitate interaction on the **Discussion Questions** that follow. (Remember: Not everyone has to offer an answer for every question.)

Leave time after your discussion to complete the **Standing Strong** exercises, which challenge each man to consider, *What's my next move?* As you openly express your thoughts to the group, you'll be able to hold one another accountable to reach for your goals.

Finally, close in **prayer**, either in your subgroups or in the larger group. You may want to use this time to reflect on and respond to what God has done in your group during the session. Also invite group members to share their personal joys and concerns, and use this as "grist" for your prayer time together.

By way of review, each lesson is divided into the following sections:

To be read or completed *before* the small-group session:
• **Key Verse**
• **Goals for Growth**
• **Head Start**
• **Connect with the Word** (home Bible study: 30-40 minutes)

To be completed *during* the small-group session:
• Read aloud the **Head Start** section (5 minutes)
• Discuss personal reaction to **Connect with the Word** (10 minutes)
• **Connect with the Group** (includes the **Group Opener** and discussion of the heart of the lesson: 30-40 minutes)
• **Standing Strong** (includes having one person pray for the group; challenges each man to take action: 20 minutes)

everyday life: no do-overs!

Have you ever wanted to rewind your life and start over? It would be like playing a country-western song backward: the dog would come home, the truck would get fixed, and the wife would return. If only it were that simple to deal with life's problems! Stuff happens, and it's not always the kind of stuff we've planned for. We certainly can't make it "un-happen."

If this is how you feel, you're not alone. You're not the only one going through tough times. This is the everyday life of the ordinary man. In fact, we're all ordinary men going through extraordinary and often painful circumstances.

In the Bible, the young David had his difficult days as well. He was perfectly happy being a shepherd boy in the countryside of Israel. Wild beasts were the greatest threat to David, but he learned to handle them. It was the rest of life that wore him down. People like King Saul constantly harassed him, and he often had to run for his life—even after he became a great national leader. Yet enemy armies were easier to deal with than family issues back home.

Can you relate? We conquer giants at work, but on the home

front, battles continue to rage. Whether we're battling with a tough marriage, an out-of-control temper, a disabling illness, or even kids gone wild, our problems often seem insurmountable.

Most of us have come to realize that every day we enter a world of circumstances that are beyond our control. (It only took us about forty years to figure that out.) What *might* go wrong *will* go wrong. (And if you don't believe us, you're still in your thirties!) The stove will break just after we fix the fridge. The car's transmission will give out just as we're agonizing over how to finance braces for the middle child. The company will decide to downsize and eliminate our department just after we've moved clear across the country for a better job and a better life.

What are you going to do about it? Are you going to fight and squirm and shake your fists at God? Are you going to demand a do-over? Or are you going to learn from everyday life and draw closer to God in tough times? The secret to coping with tough times is realizing that you can't control what happens to you. *You can only control the way you respond.*

Our study takes us through the life of David. His adventures and challenges will be our road map as we investigate how he responded to tough times.

We have discovered that most of life is lived between identifying where we want to go…and getting there. That is, life is not as much about *arriving* as it is about *traveling.* We spend most of our lives trying to get somewhere. Most men don't achieve peak performance early in life. We don't become successful in our twenties or thirties. Instead, we struggle to do our jobs, raise our kids, and make our marriages go the distance. But looking back, we find that the road we've traveled has become the substance of our lives. In David's case, he didn't just move from the hills of Palestine to a palace in Jerusalem. There was a lot of rough road in between.

Most of us want to get somewhere in life, without realizing that it will take most of our lives to get there. Few of us figure this out when we are young, nor do we arrive early. Along the way there will be plenty of rough roads—the kind God uses to do His best work in us. So David's life is a lot more like ours than we might have thought. We can learn a lot from him. He traveled the first half well.

Our goal in this study is to stimulate personal reflection and honest dialogue with God and with other men. As you work through each session, look in the mirror at your own life and ask yourself some hard questions. Whether you are doing this study individually or in a group, realize that being completely honest with yourself, with God, and with others will produce the greatest growth.

May you be moved to embrace God's plan during the tough times in a way that will leave an ongoing legacy of faith. As you do, you'll bring glory to God and hope to your brothers in Christ.

refusing to compromise

Key Verse

Now your kingdom will not endure; the LORD has sought out a man after his own heart and appointed him leader of his people, because you have not kept the LORD's command. (1 Samuel 13:14)

Goals for Growth

- Recognize that God requires obedience.
- Realize the danger of selective obedience in the heat of the moment.
- Commit to pursuing real obedience to the Lord during tough times.

Head Start

Men experience tough times; God never promised we wouldn't. And though the Bible doesn't reveal how to escape our hardships, it does show us how to get through them. James 1:2 says, "*Whenever* you face trials..." (emphasis added). So, it's not *whether* we will face tough times, but *when*.

We can learn a lot about dealing with tough times from David. First, in the midst of hardship, he didn't compromise—which says a lot about the kind of man David was. Many men cave under pressure, but David held strong. Here's what was going on at the time. Israel was involved in a religious war. The priesthood was corrupt, and the judges were dishonest and abusive. To add insult to spiritual injury, the enemy Philistines had captured the ark of the covenant. The cumulative impact this had on the people of Israel was to plunge them into spiritual darkness. They refused to listen to the prophet Samuel's warnings, and they openly rebelled against God's Word. With their eyes diverted from God, they looked at the world around them and saw what appeared to be the perfect solution: a king.

Although the prophet Samuel warned the people about the consequences of demanding a king, their tunnel vision and lack of concern for God's plan created a powerful movement to find a king. (See 1 Samuel 8.) So God gave Israel over to its careless and impatient demands and allowed the Plan B king to take the throne. This king set the stage for Israel's long and tumultuous history.

The man Samuel anointed as king was a tall, impressive, good-looking young man named Saul. This man and his exploits significantly shaped David's own destiny. In fact, we often find that Saul serves as the classic bad example when we contrast his actions with David's. Saul became David's employer, nemesis, and bounty hunter. Since David had to deal with Saul during the early years of his reign as the second anointed king of Israel, we need to understand the rival king who caused David so much grief.

As we will discover in this session, Saul typically reacted to challenges very differently than David. Instead of obeying God and refusing to compromise, he caved in and tried to engineer the circumstances to his own benefit. Sound familiar? So the big question to keep in mind as you proceed: *When times get tough, are you more like Saul or David?*

Connect with the Word

Read 1 Samuel 13:1-14.

1. Why did Saul feel "compelled" to disobey the instructions God gave through the prophet Samuel?

2. What do you think Saul's panic revealed about his relationship with God?

3. What did Saul say to Samuel when the priest confronted his disobedience?

4. In what kinds of situations today do men respond as Saul did?

5. When have you faced a time of panic or confusion like Saul did? What were your options? What did you choose to do?

6. What can a man do to prepare himself to make good choices at such times?

Read 1 Samuel 15:1-3,7-12.

7. How did Saul get "creative" with God's very clear instructions?

8. What reasoning did Saul use to convince himself to take the action he did (verse 9)?

9. What is the problem with selective obedience to God?

10. As you look at your own life, in what specific areas do you practice selective obedience to God?

11. What does verse 12 suggest about Saul's heart? Does this verse speak to your own heart right now? Explain.

12. If you were to rate yourself on the "Saul Scale" (a scale of 1 to 10: 1 = Saul and I are total opposites; 10 = Saul and I are twins), how like or unlike him would you consider yourself to be? Why

did you give yourself this rating? (*Suggestion:* Jot down some notes that you can share with your group.)

Connect with the Group

Group Opener

Read the group opener aloud and discuss the questions that follow. (Suggestion: As you begin your group discussion time in each of the following sessions, consider forming smaller groups of three to six men. This will allow more time for discussion and give everyone an opportunity to share their thoughts and struggles.)

I (Todd) worked in commercial real estate for five years right out of college. Those were good years to be in the market. Developers were buying up land faster than we could find it. Office morale was high, and most of us were making a fairly good living. On Friday afternoons we would get together for a few beers to celebrate the week. Not a big deal. As employees, we were free to choose whether or not we wanted to participate. We could stay a few minutes or a few hours. It was up to each of us. Still, not a huge deal.

The problem came when guys had a little too much to drink and called in the strippers. As a Christian I had decided ahead of time what I would participate in and what I wouldn't. I wanted to be with the guys, but I didn't want to be exposed to this kind of sin and temptation. I could handle the guys having a few too many drinks, but that's when I would leave. I didn't lead a gigantic crusade to wipe out sin in the office. My job was to manage my own obedience to the Word, and that often meant standing alone. For a season the hardship I endured was being in an environment that challenged my moral and spiritual commitment.

Discussion Questions

a. What are some of the ways you can identify with Saul's impatience and confusion as well as his decision to take matters into his own hands? (If you can, tell a personal story about this.)

b. In light of Saul's call to be king of Israel, how do you think his spiritual condition reflected the spiritual character of the nation as a whole?

c. In what way did Saul's selective obedience backfire on him?

d. In what specific ways do we, like Saul, practice selective obedience? What is God's response to us when we behave that way?

e. Like Saul, we may have a tendency to rush God. Why do we do
that? What does this say about our basic image of God? What
can we do to increase our trust in God's goodwill toward us?

Standing Strong

We've all probably noticed at least one or two tendencies in our lives that match something we saw in Saul's life. Take a moment and write down a few of these tendencies:

What first step can you take to make a change in one of these areas?

Along with the other group members, commit to carrying out your plan and be ready to share your progress at the next session.

inner character vs. outer appearances

Key Verse

The LORD said to Samuel, "Do not consider his appearance or his height, for I have rejected him. The LORD does not look at the things man looks at. Man looks at the outward appearance, but the LORD looks at the heart." (1 Samuel 16:7)

Goals for Growth

- Realize what it means that "the LORD looks at the heart."
- Recognize the importance of having a heart for God.
- Commit to developing character that pleases God.

Head Start

King Saul was a poser. When the pressure was on, in the heat of battle, his true character revealed itself. Confused and fearful, he tried to engineer circumstances by partially obeying God's clear instructions when it served his own purposes. When confronted with his disobedience, Saul justified, rationalized, and attempted to excuse his actions. His heart was dominated by arrogance toward the things of God. Tragically, we are a lot like Saul in some areas of our lives.

What a contrast David was! While Saul pursued independence from God, David longed for a deeper intimacy with Him: "I desire to do your will, O my God; your law is within my heart" (Psalm 40:8). Although David's life, like any man's, was riddled with inconsistencies, his heart remained consistently pure toward God.

As it was with David and Saul, so our conduct reflects our character, and our character reflects what is ordering our hearts. If we want to change our conduct, then our character must change. And if we want to improve our character, our hearts must be transformed. In other words, those things at the core of a man (his thoughts, feelings, motivations, priorities, values) will define him, not the image he presents to the world.

Like David, we all struggle and fail at times. Yet if we fall because of sin, we know that our standing with God remains just as it was: We are loved unconditionally, and we are perfectly accepted in Christ. But our fellowship with God can still be harmed by our sin. So, because He seeks closeness with us, God calls us out of our sin through confession and repentance and away from our self-destructive attitudes and actions—the kind that brought about Saul's downfall. (See 1 John 1:8-9.)

On the other hand, like David, we can ride out any storm if our hearts are secure in the Lord and in His love for us. As Thomas à Kempis once said, "Man weighs your actions. God weighs your intentions." As God weighs the intentions of your heart, which way is the scale tipping?

Connect with the Word

Read 1 Samuel 16:1-7; 13:14.

1. According to 1 Samuel 16:1-3, where was Samuel's focus?

2. Where was God's focus at that time?

3. Have you ever allowed the past to dominate your thinking or unduly control your decisions? Explain. What usually results from this approach to daily living?

4. What kind of man was Samuel expecting to find as he looked for God to reveal the leader He had chosen for Israel?

5. In what ways are you like Samuel, looking primarily at outward appearances? When are you most tempted to do this?

6. What is wrong with judging others by appearances? When has one of your first impressions been totally misleading or wrong?

7. What one quality in a man does God look for above all others? Why? (See 1 Samuel 13:14 and 16:7.)

8. In what ways do you think David's experiences as a shepherd helped form his heart? (See Psalms 19 and 23 for insight.)

9. Do you think David was waiting for his circumstances to change before pursuing a relationship with God? Why or why not?

10. Why do you believe David had such a pure heart before God?

11. Why do you think God's Spirit departed from Saul (1 Samuel 16:7)?

12. In the church age, the Holy Spirit permanently indwells every believer, providing leadership and guidance in the Christian life. What kinds of actions in your own life might be grieving God's Spirit right now? (See John 16:5-15 for more insight on the role of the Holy Spirit.)

Connect with the Group

Group Opener

Read the group opener aloud and discuss the questions that follow.

When I [Kenny] became a Christian in 1982, I found it relatively easy to put together the appearance of a committed follower of Christ. My days as a navy brat and my adolescent focus on appearances had taught me how to build a new image. In my high-school yearbook, there is a picture of me holding a beer mug, wearing a lampshade for a hat, and sporting a Groucho Marx nose-and-glasses disguise. The inscription underneath reads: *Life of the Party—Kenny Luck*. That was me, all right, but the caption should have read: *Best Actor Award—Kenny Luck*. You see, I was acting my buns off to get to the top of the "Most Liked" list. I learned that if I could make people laugh, they would like me—at least for a little while.

I've since learned that all men are good at creating and building images. Our single-minded, task-oriented, emotionally compartmentalized, supercompetitive, cause-and-effect, problem-solution hardwiring makes it almost inescapable. We really believe ourselves when we say, "I can do that." We find it easy to utilize the necessary appearances, props, equipment, accessories, and images so that we can project our act to the viewing audience.

Intuitive observation of how other Christians acted brought me the message that I needed to read the Bible when I became a believer in Christ—and lots and lots of pages. Most important, I had to be able to quote it....

I found the Christian fast track in no time. I became deeply involved with a Bible study group and joined an organization whose mission statement included helping fulfill the Great Commission. It wasn't long before I decided to reach for the next level by attending Fuller Theological Seminary (not far from my beloved Rose Bowl in Pasadena), and subsequent retreats and conferences drew me closer to going overseas to "serve" God. I joined a mission agency full-time, married a beautiful Christian woman, connected with and befriended other Christian couples, and began raising three kids to follow in their dad's footsteps.

Well into my Christian fast track, however, certain character flaws and inner conflicts kept this question begging in my subconscious: *Why aren't you changing for the better?...*

For most men...assembling an appearance comes naturally. It's much tougher, however, to put together a character that performs well under pressure.[1]

Discussion Questions

a. What are some of the ways we measure our own success and the success of other men? Which ways are biblical and which are not?

---

1. Stephen Arterburn and Kenny Luck, *Every Man, God's Man* (Colorado Springs: WaterBrook Press, 2003), 35-6, 37.

b. Based on the Scripture passages presented in this session, what do you think is the biggest difference between Saul and David?

c. How do you think David developed his heart for God? What can you do to develop a heart for God?

d. How do you think David kept his heart for God strong, even through all the turmoil he faced in his life? How do you keep your heart strong for God in the midst of your struggles?

e. Review the following highlights (and "lowlights") of David's life:
  • David, a shepherd boy, was anointed king of Israel (1 Samuel 16:1-13).
  • David single-handedly killed the giant Goliath (1 Samuel 17:45-51).
  • David ran in fear from King Saul (1 Samuel 19).
  • David lied and hid out with the Philistines (1 Samuel 27).
  • David became a victorious warrior (2 Samuel 8:14).

- David ruled with righteous and justice (2 Samuel 8:15).
- David committed adultery with Bathsheba (2 Samuel 11).
- David murdered Uriah (2 Samuel 11:14-26).
- David let his son attempt a coup d'état (2 Samuel 15).
- David passed on his kingdom to his son Solomon and ended his life by giving glory to God (2 Samuel 23:1-7; 1 Kings 2:1-10).

In light of David's many flaws and the horrendous sins he committed, how can we reconcile the fact that God still calls him a man after His own heart? Do you think that David's failures were just as important as his strengths in the development of his character? Why or why not?

Do you think God redeems our own failures—even our worst ones—and uses them to develop our character? Explain. If you can, share a personal example of how God has redeemed a failure in your life and used it to build godly character.

f. Since God is more concerned about the condition of our hearts than the way we appear to others, what are some practical things you can do to focus your heart on God?

Standing Strong

Based upon what you have learned, fill in the blanks any way you like:

The man after God's own heart _____.

I am going to _____ in order to develop a true heart for God.

Share with your group any practical step(s) you will take this week to develop a pure heart before God. Plan to keep your group up to date on your progress over the course of this study.

overcoming a lousy past

Key Verse

Jesse had seven of his sons pass before Samuel, but Samuel said to him, "The LORD has not chosen these." So he asked Jesse, "Are these all the sons you have?"

"There is still the youngest," Jesse answered, "but he is tending the sheep."

Samuel said, "Send for him; we will not sit down until he arrives." (1 Samuel 16:10-11)

Goals for Growth

- Recognize how David's family affected his adult life.
- Identify some family-of-origin issues that affect you today.
- Examine your heart and make decisions for ongoing change.

Head Start

I (Todd) once met a Christian real-estate agent who was driven to succeed. He eventually became one of the top ten salespeople in his company nationwide. When I asked what drove him to become so successful, he said, "As I was growing up, my dad kept telling me I'd never amount to a hill of beans. Everything I did, he criticized. Every little success I achieved, he found fault with. I determined that someday, somehow, I'd prove him wrong." He's been proving his dad wrong for thirty years.

The fact is, families form us into who we are. In the Bible, David didn't have great family encouragement either, and the lack of it affected his entire life. His family situation set him up for tough times ahead. In fact, his family was as dysfunctional as they come. His brothers constantly antagonized him, and his father neglected him. Talk about the potential for developing a poor self-image! As a result of the way his family treated him, David apparently struggled his whole life with a performance-based personality and a drive to succeed at all costs. His family left an indelible mark on his life as he gained power, influence, and significance.

Typically, our family dysfunctions drive us either to overcompensate for what is lacking in our most foundational relationships or to rely more fully upon God to take up the slack we've experienced in those relationships. For example, you may have received certain messages from your family of origin that now are contributing to patterns of sin in your life. You may hold the aching pain of loss within you, an emptiness that you seek to fill with your favorite form of escape. Many men medicate themselves daily by overworking, overeating, raging, viewing pornography, drinking alcohol, or mainlining adrenaline, to name a few common escape tactics. Yet their gnawing anxiety continues, and life remains somehow incomplete— *in spite of their high level of success.*

So now we must ask ourselves, How do we overcome the hand we've been dealt and take responsibility for our lives? How do we let our fears and anxieties move us closer to God rather than farther away? How did David do this?

Connect with the Word

Read Ruth 2:1; 4:13,17; 1 Samuel 16:1-14; 17:17-18.

1. What do you learn from Ruth 2:1 and 4:13,17 about the heritage of David's father, Jesse? Why do you think Jesse was an important man in Israel?

2. What conclusion might you draw from 1 Samuel 17:17-18 about Jesse's wealth or possibly even his ability to provide for his family? (*Hint:* Most wealthy families in Israel were measured by the productivity of their land.)

3. Though the text doesn't say, why do you think the elders "trembled" when Samuel arrived in Jesse's hometown, Bethlehem (16:4)? (*Hint:* Prophets brought either words of comfort or judgment.)

4. What do God's words in verse 7—"The LORD does not look at the things man looks at. Man looks at the outward appearance, but the LORD looks at the heart"—imply about David's brothers?

5. Compare Samuel's invitation to Jesse and his sons to come with him to sacrifice to the Lord (16:5) with verses 10-12. Where was David while Samuel was searching for God's choice to be the new king of Israel from among Jesse's own sons?

6. Why do you think Jesse did not include David when he and his other sons joined Samuel? How do you think David may have felt about being left out?

Read 1 Samuel 17:10-29.

7. What do you learn about David's father in verse 12?

8. Out of the five sons who had not gone to battle with Saul, why do you think Jesse chose David to go to the battle line with supplies and to bring back word of his three brothers who were fighting there?

9. According to verse 28, how did David's brother respond to David's questions about Goliath (verse 26)? What did Eliab's response indicate about his feelings toward David?

10. Do you think this kind of response was an isolated incident? Explain. (*Hint:* See verse 29.)

11. How would you feel about yourself if your family treated you the way David's family treated him? Explain.

12. Summarize your thoughts about the family David grew up in. Compare and contrast your own experience in your family of origin.

13. How do you think David might have felt about his family? What ongoing effects has your own family produced in you?

Connect with the Group

Group Opener

How much influence do you think families of origin have in shaping a man's outlook on life? What are some of the specific effects that dysfunctional families have upon boys as they grow into men?

Discussion Questions

a. List some of the characteristics of the family David grew up in.

b. Think of some other examples in the Bible of families that were like David's. What were the enduring effects in these families? (*Hint:* Take a look at Saul's son Jonathan in 1 Samuel 20:30. See also Samson in Judges 14:1-3 or Eli and his sons in 1 Samuel 2:32-36.)

c. What issues do you think David may have struggled with as a result of his early family experiences? What impact do you think these experiences had on him later in life?

d. What were some of the positive or negative messages about your identity and your value that you heard as a boy? What are some of the issues you have had to face because of your family upbringing?

e. Destructive family patterns are usually passed down from generation to generation. (See Numbers 14:18 and Deuteronomy 5:9.) As a husband and father, what can you do to avoid repeating the same destructive patterns that you experienced in your family of origin?

Standing Strong

What destructive pattern(s) are making life tough for you? What steps can you take to change them?

Share one old family pattern you want to change, and ask the group to pray for you this week.

overcoming the worst of circumstances

Key Verse

All those gathered here will know that it is not by sword or spear that the LORD saves; for the battle is the LORD's, and he will give all of you into our hands. (1 Samuel 17:47)

Goals for Growth

- Embrace the importance of standing up for what you believe.
- Identify the giants in your own life.
- Commit to overcoming any obstacle that paralyzes you.

Head Start

Saul, tormented and raging, found a music therapist in a shepherd boy and put him on the payroll. Just like that, David went from pasture to palace, suddenly landing in the halls of power and position. By God's design, he was able to see his own destiny begin to unfold before him.

While balancing two jobs—serving as Saul's personal harpist and tending his father's sheep—David was sent on a mission by his father. He was told to take food to his brothers at the battle front. This task changed the course of David's life and forever affected the nation of Israel.

In fact, David's mission still inspires courage in the hearts of men who feel overwhelmed, overmatched, or paralyzed by fear. The story of David and Goliath is one of the most-recounted stories in the Bible because it displays a faith and courage we all aspire to have in our own lives. Just as one man long ago conquered his fears by faith and won against all odds, we can do the same. With God all things are possible.

Every week, Kenny and I (Todd) counsel men who are struggling in life. Some are struggling with bad marriages, some with addictions, some with poor self-image, and still others with fear of the future. When we counsel them, we always start with the same question. The conversation goes something like this:

"So, how big is your God?"

"Excuse me?"

"How big is your God?"

"I don't know what you mean."

"If your God is not bigger than your problem, we can't help you."

Our point is this: If you see your problem as completely overwhelming, and you focus on it rather than on God, it will paralyze you. You need to put your problem in perspective by getting a new perspective on God. He is bigger than any problem you face. Focus on Him instead of your problem. That's what David did.

The challenge of taking on Goliath revealed that David was completely focused on the right thing: God's presence and power. In stark contrast, we see the army of Israel standing on an adjoining hillside, paralyzed with fear. Was their focus on God?

Like David, we must learn to choose faith instead of fear when facing our giants. What does such faith look like? What can we learn from David to avoid the failures of Israel?

Connect with the Word

Read 1 Samuel 16:14-23.

1. What was David's first assignment as the anointed king of Israel?

2. How do you think David might have felt about this role? What effect do you think it might have had on his sense of self-worth at this point?

Read 1 Samuel 17:1-11.

3. What does verse 11 indicate about the Israelites' state of mind at this point? What had the Israelites forgotten as they stood looking out at Goliath and the Philistine army?

4. Why do you think the Israelites didn't attack the Philistines as they had done countless times before?

Read 1 Samuel 17:20-28.

5. What was the army of Israel doing when David first arrived at the camp (verses 20 and 21)?

6. What caused the change in their confidence (verse 24)? What did the reactions of the men of Israel reveal about them?

7. What might David have been thinking in verse 26? What was his response to the situation? Why was he motivated to speak? What was David able to see that the army had missed?

8. The degree of a man's connection with God affects his fear or confidence when he faces his own giants. Have you seen this principle at work in your own life? Explain.

Read 1 Samuel 17:28-51.

9. Having dealt with the first obstacle, fear, David must contend with six other obstacles before he confronts the giant in his life. What does David do to overcome these obstacles?

criticism (verses 28 and 29)

the king (verse 33)

physical limitations (verses 33-37)

"wrong" equipment (verses 38-40)

intimidation (verses 41-44)

reality of the moment (verses 48-51)

10. What do you learn about David from verses 45-47? What does David's example teach you about your own relationship with

God? What does it teach you about how to approach the difficult situations you face today?

Read 1 Samuel 17:50-54.

11. Back in verses 11 and 24, we saw the men of Israel paralyzed by fear and unable to engage in the battle against the Philistines. What happened that motivated them into action in verse 52?

12. Who is watching you and waiting to see if you will stand up for what you say and what you believe? (See 1 Samuel 17:37.)

13. If you were willing to take steps each day to grow closer to God, what impact might it have on other people right now? Who in

your family, your place of work, or your neighborhood would be influenced by your deeper level of daily obedience?

Connect with the Group

Group Opener
Read the group opener aloud and discuss the questions that follow.

Ten years ago I (Todd) convinced my wife, Denise, to move to the Midwest for the perfect job. (I have a tip for you. If you think you've found the perfect job, you haven't. It just looks like the perfect job.) But not long after we moved away from family and close friends, I lost my job. It was the worst of circumstances. It's not what I had wanted to happen. I was crushed and confused. Then I got the bright idea of starting my own company. Five months passed with no income. Denise and I were at the end of our savings. *How bad could it get?* I thought. Then Denise became sick, and we struggled to find some answers.

I felt depressed and let down. I was frustrated with God, wondering why He had let all this happen to me. I wanted out of the situation. I wanted a better life, but it wasn't coming my way. I remember journaling during those days, asking God to be present in my time of distress. He was silent. Like Job, I was searching for the throne room of God, wanting to plead my case (Job 23).

Then one night I awoke and felt a need to open my Bible and read. I opened to Proverbs 3:5-6: "Trust in the LORD with all your heart and lean not on your own understanding; in all your ways acknowledge him, and he will make your paths straight." God was speaking to me. I could sense His presence. It was as if the lights had been out and they just came back on.

As Denise and I look back on those years, we see them as the worst of years and yet the best of years. Denise got well, I found a new job, our family grew closer, our faith grew, and we met new life-long friends who helped us through our trials.

Discussion Questions
a. If this series of events had happened to you, how would you have responded?

b. Discuss some of the different kinds of "crisis giants" men face today.

c. What have you learned from David's example that can help you face your giants in the days ahead?

d. What are the most difficult obstacles you face daily when it comes to slaying the giants in your life?

e. How have you handled these obstacles so far? In light of David's example, what steps can you take to improve the way you handle the obstacles you face?

Standing Strong

Based on what you have learned in this week's study about overcoming difficulties, complete the following statement:

The man after God's own heart _____.

What, if anything, is holding you back from standing up for God in the midst of your own personal difficulties? What steps can you take this week to begin changing this?

connecting in true friendships

Key Verse

The soul of Jonathan was knit to the soul of David, and Jonathan loved him as himself. (1 Samuel 18:1, NASB)

Goals for Growth

- Recognize the depth of David and Jonathan's friendship.
- Understand some of the reasons why men fail to enjoy deep friendships with other men.
- See the need for developing authentic male relationships and commit to doing it.

Head Start

David acquired a best friend and a worst enemy at the same time. (It just seems to happen that way—Jesus had Peter, James, and John, but he also had Judas.) Saul became David's worst enemy, hunting him down as a bird hunts down its prey. On the other hand, Jonathan, Saul's own son, became the friend who sticks closer than a brother. Jonathan even took a spear from his own father to defend his friend David against Saul. Jonathan was also the friend who challenged David to do the right things, helped him in ways no one else could, and provided a listening ear when David was in despair. Jonathan had witnessed David's victory over Goliath and saw David as someone he admired and wanted to know.

At the same time, Jonathan knew intuitively that David was destined to replace his father on the throne. He knew that he himself would not be the one to rule Israel, yet he didn't wait to start serving the king-in-waiting. Like David, Jonathan was bold and aggressive, and he maintained a strong relationship with God. No wonder the text tells us that their hearts were chained together! (See 1 Samuel 20:42.)

The friendship between Jonathan and David is one of the strongest man-to-man relationships recorded in the Bible. The bond between them was rooted in their commitment to God. It grew stronger when tested, and it could not be broken by circumstances or even the threat of death. Even though David was a man after God's own heart, God still wanted him to have friendships with others. God is enough, but He still chooses to use others to speak to us, comfort us, and guide us. In a sense, God revealed Himself to David wrapped in the skin of his friend, Jonathan. Did David need Jonathan? Absolutely. Tough times require close friends close by.

Connect with the Word

Read 1 Samuel 18:1-4; 19:1-7.

1. What do you think Jonathan saw in David that made him want to be David's friend?

2. What does it mean that the soul of Jonathan was "knit" to David's? If our hearts were knit together with God's heart, what impact would that have on our relationship with Him?

3. What does it mean to love someone as you love yourself? In what ways would loving someone as yourself change the dynamics of your friendship? (See 1 Peter 1:22.)

4. What was the significance of Jonathan's giving David his sword and other belongings?

5. What do you learn from these passages about how God's purposes are fulfilled through people who strongly influence our lives?

Read 1 Samuel 20:1-4.

6. What do you think David needed most from Jonathan at this point in his life?

7. After David expressed his confusion and disappointment to Jonathan, how do you think David felt about Jonathan's response in verse 4?

8. What guidance do you find from Jonathan's actions to help you know how to respond to a crisis in another man's life?

Read 1 Samuel 20:12-34.

9. How did Jonathan go the extra mile for his friend? What risks was he likely taking?

10. What does verse 23 suggest as the basis for confidence in their friendship?

11. How did Jonathan honor God, his father, and David in the confrontation with Saul in verses 28-34?

Read 1 Samuel 20:35-42.

12. What is your reaction to the expressions of love and deep emotion between David and Jonathan in verse 41? Do your friends allow you the freedom to be transparent and openly share your emotions without making you feel weird or judged? Do you give

your friends the same freedom? How can you improve in this area?

13. Sometimes the pressures on a man are enough to make him cry, but most of us would never let other men see our emotions. What prevents this kind of openness among men? Where do we go with our emotions? Where *should* we go with them?

14. Why do you think David grieved so intensely about leaving his friend? What do Jonathan's words in verse 42 suggest about God's purpose for our friendships?

Connect with the Group

Group Opener
Read the group opener aloud and discuss the questions that follow.

Recently I (Todd) underwent a battery of medical tests to determine the cause of severe stomach pain. I feared the worst. An upper G.I. test revealed some kind of inflammation in the intestines. There was also a spot on my spine that looked odd. Nothing is worse than news like that. I lost about seven pounds and became so overwhelmed by fear that I closed up and sealed myself off from others.

During that week of tests, a friend came over to the house to see how I was doing. Since I hadn't reached out, he reached out to me. You always know who your friends are. They're the ones who never give up on you.

Paul and I sat in my office, and he just fired away. "Hey, Todd, how come you're not reaching out and letting your friends stand with you during this time? You and Kenny are writing all this curriculum about how men need to be connected with other men, and here you are isolated! How come you're shutting out your best friends when you need them most?"

Yikes! Did he really say that? But he was right. I had called some of my friends to let them know what was going on, but I hadn't really included them in the process. It was too painful. I didn't want to talk about it. I wanted it to just go away.

Discussion Questions

a. Why do you think men typically shy away from having a relationship with another man like the one David had with Jonathan? (See Proverbs 18:24.)

b. What do the following say about David and Jonathan's friendship?

"knit" soul (1 Samuel 18:1, NASB)

"loved" (1 Samuel 18:1,13, NASB)

"delighted in" or "very fond of" (1 Samuel 19:1)

"wept" (1 Samuel 20:41)

"kissed" (1 Samuel 20:41)

c. Why would this list tend to make some men uncomfortable? Why do you think we struggle with such descriptions of a relationship between men?

d. What might it cost you to build a relationship like this with another man? (See 1 Samuel 20:4,13.)

e. Are you willing to be accountable to your friends? Why or why not?

f. To whom can you say what Jonathan said to David in 1 Samuel 20:4?

Standing Strong

Complete the following sentence:

The man after God's own heart experiences God's love through

_____.

Appropriate and intimate friendships are based upon an abiding relationship with the Lord. How open are you to intimacy with God? Explain. What can you do to surrender your heart more fully to Him—to let Him know the "real you"?

What specific steps can you take to begin developing a close friendship? Remember, you don't just wake up one day and have a Jonathan in your life! It takes time. What else does it take?

Step 1: _____

Step 2: _____

Step 3: _____

Step 4: _____

Step 5: _____

Step 6: _____

choosing not to retaliate

Key Verse

The LORD is near to the brokenhearted and saves those who are crushed in spirit. Many are the afflictions of the righteous, but the LORD delivers him out of them all. (Psalm 34:18-19, NASB)

Goals for Growth

- Recognize that God allows difficulties in our lives for a purpose.
- Learn to trust God more fully during tough times.
- Surrender your life fully to the Lord in every circumstance.

Head Start

His boss was growing increasingly unpredictable, eventually becoming deranged and murderous. But David chose restraint in the face of

Saul's raging fits. As an accomplished warrior, David could have fought back. But he chose not to do that. What was the key to his tolerance of Saul's hatred?

In 1 Samuel 18–20 we read of Saul's passive-aggressive behavior as well as his overt acts of violence as he let his jealousy of David run out of control. But in spite of this, David continued to serve his king, taking every opportunity to please him. However, when Saul hurled his spear at David again and missed, David's naive notions about winning Saul over must have been dashed. Yet instead of retaliating, he retreated. David, the victorious war hero, ran from a single enemy!

What would you have done? Would you have retaliated? Or, more to the point, what do you do today when a perceived enemy hurls a spear in your direction? How does a tough trial affect your faith in God? Not an easy question to answer, right? *What's God up to? Doesn't He know it's me? This was not my plan!*

Like David, we all learn that God's plan often involves delays and difficulties that can provide the experience and develop the character we need for the next step in our spiritual growth. God doesn't waste anything in our lives. Every event is an instrument to make us more like Christ—*if* we let it be that.

David went from hero, to bigger hero, to zero—for no logical reason other than Saul's jealousy and pride. Although at times David must have felt as if God were asleep on the job, He was actually at work in David's character, preparing him for the ultimate comeback. That's why, when spears start to fly, it's usually best to run for cover and not retaliate—even for men after God's own heart.

Connect with the Word

For background, read 1 Samuel 18–21. (*Note:* Saul's attacks: 1 Samuel 18:11,21,29; 19:10; 20:33. David's responses: 1 Samuel 18:30; 19:2,12,18; 20:1; 21:2,10,13; 22:1.)

1. David said, "What have I done? What is my crime? How have I wronged your father, that he is trying to take my life?" (1 Samuel 20:1). What were the answers to David's questions? How did David respond to Saul's attacks? How *could* he have responded?

2. What doubts might have been created in David's mind about God's promise regarding his future as king of Israel? Samuel had anointed young David as king, but at the moment, this didn't appear to be a promising reality. What purpose might God have had in allowing this difficulty with Saul to arise in David's life?

3. During his life, David sometimes took a few steps forward, and then a few steps back. How do you see David's faith holding up under the pressure of Saul's attacks? Take a brief look at 1 Samuel 24:1-12. What may have motivated David's choices?

4. How did being a fugitive help prepare David for his future as king? What lessons did he learn as a fugitive that success, victories, and royal employment could not teach him?

5. What happens to a man when he reaches the end of his ability to control a situation? (See Matthew 5:3.)

6. In what ways did David glorify God during his years as a fugitive? (*Hint:* He recorded his innermost thoughts and struggles in words and music in a certain book of the Bible.)

Read Psalm 34.

7. According to verse 4, what did David do and what was God's response?

8. How did David integrate his relationship with God into his trial (verses 1-6)?

9. What do you see in David's example that should characterize your own prayer life when trials and crises strike?

10. According to verse 18, where is God when we are under a lot of pressure or are in crisis?

11. What truths gave David strength and helped him persevere (verses 19-22)?

Connect with the Group

Group Opener

Describe a time in your life when you felt pursued by an "enemy"— a boss, a spouse, a friend, a coworker or partner, or even the real McCoy.

Discussion Questions

a. If you were David, how would you have responded to Saul's attacks?

b. How do you typically respond when you are unfairly put down, or—worse—when your motives are impugned? Give an example, if you can.

c. Do you think it is ever right to run in fear? When have you had to run? How did things turn out? What role did God play in that situation?

d. What did David's lying and deception reveal about his faith in this situation? (See 1 Samuel 21:10-13.) When have you tried to take matters into your own hands for self-preservation? Explain. How did things turn out?

e. What specific principles can we learn from David about how to handle personal attacks?

Standing Strong

Write down some unhealthy ways you respond in tough times. Be aware of these tendencies this week and give them over to the Lord.

Based on what you've just studied, complete the following statement:

The man after God's own heart _____.

identifying your fear

Key Verse

Once again David inquired of the LORD, and the LORD answered him. (1 Samuel 23:4)

Goals for Growth

- Recognize the signs of David's failure to trust God.
- Realize the consequences of deception and lies.
- Turn to the Lord first, and call out to Him for help.

Head Start

David was running scared. But was he so different from us? We tend to do that when our circumstances are out of control and closing in on us. Like us, David got "creative" in a couple of ways that ran counter to God's plan.

It's called compromise. Under stress David resorted to the quick fixes of deception over honesty and trusting in human intelligence over God's wisdom. But while convenient, these quick fixes were catastrophic to his walk with God. First, David turned to the high priest, Ahimelech, and instead of being honest about his true needs and intentions, he lied.

Then it got worse: David faked mental illness in order to gain protection from a king he had previously attempted to kill. Fear made him do strange things—things he shouldn't have been doing. David even lied to a brother, and then turned to the enemy for help. Fear led David to sin instead of driving him to God. Yet, in the end, we see David come to his senses. He finally did what he should have done at first: he "inquired of the LORD" (1 Samuel 23:2). He stopped acting out of fear and started acting out of faith.

Up to this point, David had been on a path leading to the top of the "career" ladder. He had been anointed as future king, he had defeated a legendary enemy, he had become a legend himself, and he was added to the royal payroll on a fast track to the throne. David was held in high esteem in Israel, and he enjoyed enormous potential for greatness. But he also had the potential to cave in under the pressure of his circumstances.

In fact, God's training of the king-in-waiting was just beginning. God did deliver David miraculously from the lion when he was shepherding sheep and, later, from the hand of Goliath. But faith and character were not delivered by priority mail to David's front porch. These would be forged in the fugitive years when he was stretched to the limit in every way. God taught David to trust Him, and He developed his character in the crucible of obstacles, delays, and heartbreaks.

How does pressure test a man's character? When or where will you bend, fudge, twist, or manipulate the rules to save your skin (or your image)? When do you find yourself living out of fear?

Connect with the Word

Read 1 Samuel 21:1-9.

1. What dilemma did the high priest Ahimelech face when David asked for bread? What higher law do you think governed Ahimelech's decision to give the consecrated bread to David? (See Matthew 12:1-8.)

2. Why do you think David lied to the priest? What should he have done?

3. In situations like David's, what does it take to win in a way that pleases God? When have you won—or lost—under a similar kind of pressure?

Read 1 Samuel 21:10-14.

4. Why do you think David ran to the enemy? How did the plan backfire?

5. Under what kinds of high-pressure situations are you tempted to resort to lies or deceit? What are some outcomes of taking this course of action?

6. In what ways has God upheld and supported you in these situations?

Read 1 Samuel 22.

7. What resulted from David's lies? Do you think David realized he was putting Ahimelech at risk when he went to him for help? Explain.

8. What are some ways you have put others at risk to save your own skin? What would give you more courage in the future?

Read 1 Samuel 23.

9. In 1 Samuel 23:1, David was told about the Philistine attack on Keilah. What was David's response to the situation (verse 2)? When you are desperate, to whom do you naturally turn for relief?

10. What do David's actions in verses 2, 4, and 9-12 reveal about his thinking at this point? In what ways did his approach here differ from his reactions in the previous situations?

11. According to verses 7 and 8, how did Saul interpret and manage the same events?

12. Have you ever responded the way David did in this situation? the way Saul did? Explain, and give examples, if possible.

13. The crisis went to the next level in verses 9-11. According to verses 15-18, how was David's obedience under pressure rewarded?

14. How did Jonathan help David "find strength" to persevere (verses 16-18)?

15. According to verses 26-29, what was God's ultimate provision for David in the midst of this crisis?

Connect with the Group

Group Opener
Read the group opener aloud and discuss the questions that follow.

[God] knows us. He knows that most men will not change until the pain of their circumstances exceeds the pain of change. For Chris [Kenny's brother], it was months and months of living as a slave to his appetites for women and partying. In my case, it was going twenty thousand dollars in debt. For others, it could be:

- a job layoff
- a business failure
- a pregnant daughter who just turned sixteen
- the discovery of cancerous nodes
- the death of a child
- a wife who coldly announces that the marriage is over
- the loss of a dream[2]

Discussion Questions
a. How do you respond to the quote above? With what do you agree? disagree? How might you say it differently?

---

2. Stephen Arterburn and Kenny Luck, *Every Man, God's Man* (Colorado Springs: WaterBrook Press, 2003), 42.

b. Share a story that illustrates how you typically respond in times of crisis.

c. David found himself in situations that forced him to either find his own way out or put his trust in God. How did he respond in each of the following circumstances?

after Jonathan sent him away (1 Samuel 19:1-7)

when he went to Ahimelech (1 Samuel 20:35–21:6)

when he went to Gath (1 Samuel 21:10-15)

before he went to save Keilah (1 Samuel 23:1-6)

when he learned of Saul's plot to find him in Keilah (1 Samuel 23:9-12)

d. What brought about the change in David's approach to fearful situations?

e. According to 1 Samuel 23:14-18 and 24-29, how did God meet David's needs?

f. What has kept you personally from being truthful in a time of self-preservation? What would help you become more trusting of—and reliant upon—God's direction and help at those times?

g. Share about a time when you sought the Lord in the midst of your trouble and He provided help or a way out. What key lesson(s) did you learn during that time? In what ways did you grow in Christian maturity?

Standing Strong

Based on this week's study, complete the statement below to reflect the man you believe God wants you to be.

The man after God's own heart _____.

What would it take for you to loosen your grip—to become less control-oriented—in future crisis situations? To what extent will this require changing your perspective of God so that you see Him as completely loving and on your side?

swimming against the current

Key Verse

This day you have seen with your own eyes how the LORD delivered you into my hands in the cave. Some urged me to kill you, but I spared you; I said, "I will not lift my hand against my master, because he is the LORD's anointed." (1 Samuel 24:10)

Goals for Growth

- Recognize how we can stand alone for God when it seems easier to do otherwise.
- Realize that our strength in difficulty comes from living according to God's ways.
- See the benefits of living to please God.

Head Start

Imagine being hunted like an animal. You're on the run. Then, out of nowhere, your hunter is handed to you on a silver platter. He can't see you, but you see him! He's standing in front of you, and you've got him right in the cross hairs. Your misery and pain could be over with one pull of the trigger, and no one would ever blame you. In fact, everyone around you is egging you on to end it all here and now.

Imagine, too, that you have justifiable cause to retaliate. You have been wronged, and it's payback time. You would be hailed as a hero and promoted to the top position in the land, and you would begin a new life of plenty and power. Your future is, literally and figuratively, in your hands. You feel serious pressure inside, and even greater pressure from the outside, to *just pull that trigger.*

What would you do?

David's encounters, as a fugitive, with Saul move us to ask ourselves some important questions: Am I really the master of my own fate? Can I indeed engineer my future so that everything turns out just the way I want it to? If the opportunity arises to even the odds, does that mean I should seize it?

No matter how we answer such questions (and a million more like them), each believer is called to listen for God and respond to His will against the strong pull of fleshly desires and the pressures of the crowd. Ultimately, being God's man in tough times is about standing for what is right, even if it means standing alone.

Connect with the Word

Read 1 Samuel 24.

1. According to verses 1 and 2, what were Saul's intentions regarding David? What was he planning on doing with three thousand

men? Was David outnumbered? (See 1 Samuel 23:13; 24:2; 26:2, and 27:2.)

2. When David's men discovered Saul in the cave, how did they encourage David to respond (verses 3 and 4)? What did David do instead? What do Proverbs 3:5-6 and 14:12 say about the action David took?

3. How did David feel after cutting off the corner of Saul's robe (verse 5)? What explanation did David offer his men for not killing Saul (verses 6 and 7)?

4. According to verses 8-15, how did David deal with Saul after he left the cave?

5. What do David's actions reveal about his character and his commitment to God? What do you think God was doing in David's life here?

6. How significant is it for you that David took this course of action in spite of what his men felt he should have done? Explain. In what ways do Deuteronomy 32:35 and Romans 12:19 affirm David's actions?

7. What did Saul's response and lament suggest about his view of David? What did his response reveal about himself (verse 17)?

8. David stood alone for what he believed was right. How was he rewarded for not retaliating (verses 16-22)?

Read 1 Samuel 26:1–27:4.

9. When David found himself under intense pressure to kill Saul again, what reason did he give for not doing it (verses 9-11)?

10. List some of the benefits of trusting in God's will and timing instead of taking matters into your own hands. (See Matthew 26:36-39.)

11. Why do you think God gave David a second opportunity to kill Saul?

12. According to verses 23-24, what was shaping David's thinking as he confronted Saul?

13. In the end, whom do you think God viewed as the most honorable man, Saul or David? Why?

14. Although David honored Saul by showing him kindness and mercy, do you think David's actions in 1 Samuel 27:1-4 showed wisdom or a lack of faith? Explain.

Connect with the Group

Group Opener

Put yourself in the situation of one who has just been mistreated on the job. How do men typically respond when they are mistreated? Can you share an example from your own life?

Discussion Questions

a. What character qualities was God trying to produce in David?

b. Give some examples of situations where we can refuse to retaliate even though circumstances suggest that we would be totally justified.

c. Discuss the differences you noticed in this study between Saul's mind-set and David's.

d. What did Jesus teach about our enemies in Matthew 5:43-47? How does this passage relate to David and Saul?

Standing Strong

Complete the sentence below with a statement about how this study has helped you know what it means to please God day by day.

The man after God's own heart _____.

What circumstances in your life might be better resolved if you showed some kindness or forgiveness rather than retaliation? What specifically can you do? Make a plan and share it with your group.

concluding exercise

Reflect on what you've learned in this study, and describe what God has taught you about how to deal with tough times. Write a short journal entry describing your initial feelings and how your perspective has changed as a result of studying the Word of God.

small-group resources

leader tips

What if men aren't doing the Connect with the Word section before our small-group session?

Don't be discouraged. You set the pace. If you are doing the study and regularly referring to it in conversations with your men through-out the week, they will pick up on its importance. Here are some suggestions to motivate the men in your group to do their home Bible study:

- Send out a midweek e-mail in which you share your answer to one of the study questions. This shows them that you are personally committed to and involved in the study.
- Ask the guys to hit "respond to all" on their e-mail program and share one insight from that week's Bible study with the entire group. Encourage them to send it out before the next small-group session.
- Every time you meet, ask each man in the group to share one insight from his home study.

What if men are not showing up for small group?

This might mean they are losing a sin battle and don't want to admit it to the group. Or they might be consumed with other priorities. Or maybe they don't think they're getting anything out of the group. Here are some suggestions for getting the guys back each week:

- Affirm them when they show up, and tell them how much it means to you that they make small group a priority.

- From time to time, ask them to share one reason they think small group is important to them.
- Regularly call or send out an e-mail the day before you meet to remind them you're looking forward to seeing them.
- Check in with any guy who has missed more than one session, and find out what's going on in his life.
- Get some feedback from the men. You may need to adjust your style. Listen and learn.

What if group discussion is not happening?

You are a discussion facilitator. You have to keep guys involved in the discussion or you'll lose them. You can engage a man who isn't sharing by saying, "Chuck, you've been quiet. What do you think about this question or discussion?" You should also be prepared to share your own personal stories that are related to the discussion questions. You'll set the example by the kind of sharing you do.

What if one man is dominating the group time?

You have to deal with it. If you don't, men will stop showing up. No one wants to hear from just one guy all the time. It will quickly kill morale. Meet with the guy in person and privately. Firmly but gently suggest that he allow others more time to talk. Be positive and encouraging, but truthful. You might say, "Bob, I notice how enthusiastic you are about the group and how you're always prepared to share your thoughts with the group. But there are some pretty quiet guys in the group too. Have you noticed? Would you be willing to help me get them involved in speaking up?"

How do I get the guys in my group more involved?

Give them something to do. Ask one guy to bring a snack. Invite another to lead the prayer time (ask in advance). Have one guy sub for you one week as the leader. (Meet with him beforehand to walk through the group program and the time allotments for each segment.) Encourage another guy to lead a subgroup.

What if guys are not being vulnerable during the Standing Strong or prayer times?

You model openness. You set the pace. Honesty breeds honesty. Vulnerability breeds vulnerability. Are you being vulnerable and honest about your own problems and struggles? (This doesn't mean that you have to spill your guts each week or reveal every secret of your life.) Remember, men want an honest, on their-level leader who strives to walk with God. (Also, as the leader, you need an accountability partner, perhaps another group leader.)

What will we do at the first session?

We encourage you to open by discussing the **Small-Group Covenant** we've included in this resource section. Ask the men to commit to the study, and then discuss how long it will take your group to complete each session. (We suggest 75-90 minute sessions.) Men find it harder to come up with excuses for missing a group session if they have made a covenant to the other men right at the start.

Begin to identify ways certain men can play a more active role in small group. Give away responsibility. You won't feel as burdened, and your men will grow from the experience. Keep in mind that this process can take a few weeks. Challenge men to fulfill one of the group roles identified later in this resource section. If no one steps forward to fill a role, say to one of the men, "George, I've noticed that you are comfortable praying in a group. Would you lead us each week during that time?"

How can we keep the group connected after we finish a study?
Begin talking about starting another Bible study before you finish this eight-week study. (There are six studies to choose from in the Every Man Bible study series.) Consider having a social time at the conclusion of the study, and encourage the men to invite a friend. This will help create momentum and encourage growth as you launch into another study with your group. There are probably many men in your church or neighborhood who aren't in small groups but would like to be. Be the kind of group that includes others.

As your group grows, consider choosing an apprentice leader who can take half the group into another room for the **Connect with the Group** time. That subgroup can stay together for prayer, or you can reconvene as a large group during that time. You could also meet for discussion as a large group, and then break into subgroups for **Standing Strong** and **prayer**.

If your group doubles in size, it might be a perfect opportunity to release your apprentice leader with half the group to start another group. Allow men to pray about this and make a decision as a group. Typically, the relational complexities that come into play when a small group births a new group work themselves out. Allow guys to choose which group they'd like to be a part of. If guys are slow in choosing one group or another, ask them individually to select one of the groups. Take the lead in making this happen.

Look for opportunities for your group to serve in the church or community. Consider a local outreach project or a short-term missions trip. There are literally hundreds of practical ways you can serve the Lord in outreach. Check with your church leaders to learn the needs in your congregation or community. Create some interest by sending out scouts who will return with a report for the group. Serving keeps men from becoming self-focused and ingrown. When you serve as a group, you will grow as a group.

using this study in a large-group format

Many church leaders are looking for biblically based curriculum that can be used in a large-group setting, such as a Sunday-school class, or for small groups within an existing larger men's group. Each of the Every Man Bible studies can be adapted for this purpose. In addition, this curriculum can become a catalyst for churches wishing to launch men's small groups or to build a men's ministry in their church.

Getting Started

Begin by getting the word out to men in your church, inviting them to join you for a men's study based on one of the topics in the Every Man Bible study series. You can place a notice in your church bulletin, have the pastor announce it from the pulpit, or pursue some other means of attracting interest.

Orientation Week

Arrange your room with round tables and chairs. Put approximately six chairs at each table.

Start your class in prayer and introduce your topic with a short but motivational message from any of the scriptures used in the Bible study. Hand out the curriculum and challenge the men to do their homework before each class. During this first session give the men some discussion questions based upon an overview of the material and have them talk things through just within their small group around the table.

Just before you wrap things up, have each group select a table host or leader. You can do this by having everyone point at once to the person at their table they feel would best facilitate discussion for future meetings.

Ask those newly elected table leaders to stay after for a few minutes, and offer them an opportunity to be further trained as small-group leaders as they lead discussions throughout the course of the study.

Subsequent Weeks

Begin in prayer. Then give a short message (15-25 minutes) based upon the scripture used for that lesson. Pull out the most motivating topics or points and strive to make the discussion relevant to the life of an everyday man and his world. Then leave time for each table to work through the discussion questions listed in the curriculum. Be sure the discussion facilitators at each table close in prayer.

At the end of the eight sessions, you might want to challenge each "table group" to become a small group, inviting them to meet regularly with their new small-group leader and continue building the relationships they've begun.

prayer request record

Date:
Name:
Prayer Request:
Praise:

Date:
Name:
Prayer Request:
Praise:

Date:
Name:
Prayer Request:
Praise:

Date:
Name:
Prayer Request:
Praise:

Date:
Name:
Prayer Request:
Praise:

defining group roles

Group Leader: Leads the lesson and facilitates group discussion.

Apprentice Leader: Assists the leader as needed, which may include leading the lesson.

Refreshment Coordinator: Maintains a list of who will provide refreshments. Calls group members on the list to remind them to bring what they signed up for.

Prayer Warrior: Serves as the contact person for prayer between sessions. Establishes a list of those willing to pray for needs that arise. Maintains the prayer-chain list and activates the chain as needed by calling the first person on the list.

Social Chairman: Plans any desired social events during group sessions or at another scheduled time. Gathers members for planning committees as needed.

small-group roster

Name:
Address:
Phone: E-mail:

Name:
Address:
Phone: E-mail:

Name:
Address:
Phone: E-mail:

Name:
Address:
Phone: E-mail:

Name:
Address:
Phone: E-mail:

Name:
Address:
Phone: E-mail:

spiritual checkup

Your answers to the statements below will help you determine which areas you need to work on in order to grow spiritually. Mark the appropriate letter to the left of each statement. Then make a plan to take one step toward further growth in each area. Don't forget to pray for the Lord's wisdom before you begin. Be honest. Don't be overly critical or rationalize your weaknesses.

> **Y** = Yes
> **S** = Somewhat or Sometimes
> **N** = No

My Spiritual Connection with Other Believers

____I am developing relationships with Christian friends.

____I have joined a small group.

____I am dealing with conflict in a biblical manner.

____I have become more loving and forgiving than I was a year ago.

____I am a loving and devoted husband and father.

My Spiritual Growth

____I have committed to daily Bible reading and prayer.

____I am journaling on a regular basis, recording my spiritual growth.

____I am growing spiritually by studying the Bible with others.

____I am honoring God in my finances and personal giving.

____I am filled with joy and gratitude for my life, even during trials.

____I respond to challenges with peace and faith instead of anxiety and anger.

____I avoid addictive behaviors (excessive drinking, overeating, watching too much TV, etc.).

Serving Christ and Others

____I am in the process of discovering my spiritual gifts and talents.

____I am involved in ministry in my church.

____I have taken on a role or responsibility in my small group.

____I am committed to helping someone else grow in his spiritual walk.

Sharing Christ with Others

____I care about and am praying for those around me who are unbelievers.

____I share my experience of coming to know Christ with others.

____I invite others to join me in this group or for weekend worship services.

____I am seeing others come to Christ and am praying for this to happen.

____I do what I can to show kindness to people who don't know Christ.

Surrendering My Life for Growth

___I attend church services weekly.

___I pray for others to know Christ, and I seek to fulfill the Great Commission.

___I regularly worship God through prayer, praise, and music, both at church and at home.

___I care for my body through exercise, nutrition, and rest.

___I am concerned about using my energy to serve God's purposes instead of my own.

My Identity in the Lord

___I see myself as a beloved son of God, one whom God loves regardless of my sin.

___I can come to God in all of my humanity and know that He accepts me completely. When I fail, I willingly run to God for forgiveness.

___I experience Jesus as an encouraging Friend and Lord each moment of the day.

___I have an abiding sense that God is on my side. I am aware of His gracious presence with me throughout the day.

___During moments of beauty, grace, and human connection, I lift up praise and thanks to God.

___I believe that using my talents to their fullest pleases the Lord.

___I experience God's love for me in powerful ways.

small-group covenant

As a committed group member, I agree to the following:*

- **Regular Attendance.** I will attend group sessions on time and let everyone know in advance if I can't make it.
- **Group Safety.** I will help create a safe, encouraging environment where men can share their thoughts and feelings without fear of embarrassment or rejection. I will not judge another guy or attempt to fix his problems.
- **Confidentiality.** I will always keep to myself everything that is shared in the group.
- **Acceptance.** I will respect different opinions or beliefs and let Scripture be the teacher.
- **Accountability.** I will make myself accountable to the other group members for the personal goals I share.
- **Friendliness.** I will look for those around me who might join the group and explore their faith with other men.
- **Ownership.** I will prayerfully consider taking on a specific role within the group as the opportunity arises.
- **Spiritual Growth.** I will commit to establishing a daily quiet time with God, which includes doing the homework for this study. I will share with the group the progress I make and the struggles I experience as I seek to grow spiritually.

Signed: _____ Date: _____

---

* *Permission is given to photocopy and distribute this form to each man in your group. Review this covenant quarterly or as needed.*

about the authors

 STEPHEN ARTERBURN is coauthor of the best-selling Every Man series. He is also founder and chairman of New Life Clinics, host of the daily *New Life Live!* national radio program, and creator of the Women of Faith conferences. A nationally known speaker and licensed minister, Stephen has authored more than forty books. He lives with his family in Laguna Beach, California.

 KENNY LUCK is president and founder of Every Man Ministries and coauthor of *Every Man, God's Man* and its companion workbook. He is division leader for men's small groups and teaches a men's interactive Bible study at Saddleback Church in Lake Forest, California. He and his wife, Chrissy, have three children and reside in Rancho Santa Margarita, California.

 TODD WENDORFF is a graduate of U.C. Berkeley and holds a Th.M. from Talbot School of Theology. He serves as a pastor of men's ministries at Saddleback Church and is an adjunct professor at Biola University. He is an author of the Doing Life Together Bible study series. Todd and his wife, Denise, live with their three children in Trabuco Canyon, California.

every man's battle
workshops
from New Life Ministries

new Life Ministries receives hundreds of calls every month from Christian men who are struggling to stay pure in the midst of daily challenges to their sexual integrity and from pastors who are looking for guidance in how to keep fragile marriages from falling apart all around them.

As part of our commitment to equip individuals to win these battles, New Life Ministries has developed biblically based workshops directly geared to answer these needs. These workshops are held several times per year around the country.

- Our workshops **for men** are structured to equip men with the tools necessary to maintain sexual integrity and enjoy healthy, productive relationships.

- Our workshops **for church leaders** are targeted to help pastors and men's ministry leaders develop programs to help families being attacked by this destructive addiction.

Some comments from previous workshop attendees:

"An awesome, life-changing experience. Awesome teaching, teacher, content and program." —DAVE

"God has truly worked a great work in me since the EMB workshop. I am fully confident that with God's help, I will be restored in my ministry position. Thank you for your concern. I realize that this is a battle, but I now have the weapons of warfare as mentioned in Ephesians 6:10, and I am using them to gain victory!" —KEN

"It's great to have a workshop you can confidently recommend to anyone without hesitation, knowing that it is truly life changing. Your labors are not in vain!" —DR. BRAD STENBERG, Pasadena, CA

If sexual temptation is threatening your marriage or your church, please call **1-800-NEW-LIFE** to speak with one of our specialists.

every man conferences
revolutionizing local churches

"This is a revolutionary conference that has the potential to change the world. Thanks Kenny! The fire is kindled!" —B.J.

"The conference was tremendous and exactly what I needed personally. The church I pastor is starting a men's group to study the material launched at this conference. This is truly an answer to my prayer!" —DAVID

"Thank you! Thank you! Thank you! I didn't know how much I needed this. I look forward to working through the material with my small group." —BOB

"It's the only conference I have attended where I will go back and read my notes!" —ROGER

"This is a conference every man should attend." —KARL

"After years of waffling with God, I am ready to welcome Him into my every day life. Thanks for giving me the tools to help me develop a relationship with God." —GEORGE

"This revolutionary conference is the next wave of men's ministry in America." —STEVE ARTERBURN, Coauthor of *Every Man's Battle*

If you want to :
- **address the highest felt need issues among men**
- **launch or grow your men's ministry**
- **connect your men in small groups around God's Word**
- **and reach seeking men with the Gospel**

Join with other churches or sponsor an every man conference in your area.

For information on booking Kenny Luck or scheduling an Every Man Conference contact Every Man Ministries at 949-766-7830 or email at everymanministries@aol.com. For more information on Every Man events, visit our website at everymanministries.com.

start a bible study
and connect with others
who want to be God's man.

Every Man Bible Studies are designed to help you discover, own, and build
on convictions grounded in God's word. Available now in bookstores.

WATERBROOK
PRESS

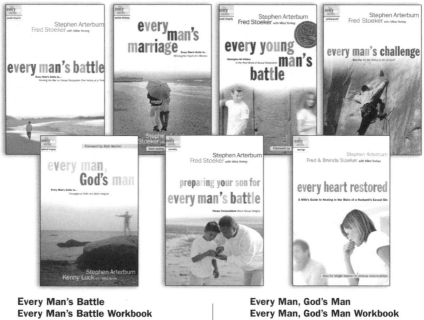